QUIET TIME

WHAT, WHEN
WITH WHOM
WHY, HOW
&
HEARING FROM GOD

A LIFE-LONG TOUR WITH GOD

Samuel Jimson Olorunfemi

Published by

God's Triumphant Faith Publications

AnuOluwa Estate, Alapo, Olorunda-Abaa
After Akobo-Ojurin Bus Stop, Akobo,
Ibadan, Oyo State, Nigeria, West Africa
Box 21281, U.I. Post Office, Ibadan
E-mail: sajorev7@yahoo.com
Tel: + 234 803 562 4406, + 234 805 530 1639
+ 234 806 637 1796
E-mail: sajorev7@yahoo.com

First published 1998
Revised and Reprinted 2-15
Reprinted 2020

ISBN 979-8846441392

Unless otherwise indicated scripture quotations are from the King James Version of the Holy Bible.

Contents

Dedication

Dedicated to the living memory of the spirit of benevolence which was manifested in my beloved mum, Elizabeth Olorunfemi (Nee Amoni) during her life-time and same that is also being manifested in my respected uncle, Prof. S.S. Amoni; and ultimately to the Almighty God who is identified by the name 'Benevolence', from whom all help comes.

Preface

The phrase, "Quiet Time" is a slogan in Christianity which its meaning yet eludes so man, in the faith, that
Gods people.

However, in this compass, the term, 'Quiet Time' is elucidated. Its dynamism is unveiled, while its inevitability to any bonafide child, son or daughter of God, who desires a good beginning and better ending in Christian walk, business, life and ministry is made bare.

My sincere heartfelt prayer and belief is that your life will experience a remarkable turning as you meditatively study this supernatural life-booster; in Jesus's mighty name (Amen).

Rev (Barrister) Samuel Jimson Olorunfemi
Ibadan

Chapter One

Introduction

The phrase 'Quiet Time' is simply adopted in this work with a view to expressing a time or period that a person (man or woman) consciously, conscientiously and incumbently separates to spend alone with God, without allowing any distractions whatsoever from any quarter.

It is a period dedicated to remaining in a close circuit, alone with God, shut out of every distraction, with the motive to knowing Him on a progressive basis, having for preparedness, a heart that is determined to thanking and praising God; searching, studying and meditating in the scriptures, as well as communing with Him in prayers and hearing from Him.

With the latter revelation above, it is pertinent to acknowledge that the subject, "Quiet Time" is for all level of Christians, from childhood to adulthood; a newly-born one or old, a lay Christian or Minister of the Gospel and from an inexperienced level to a stage of perfection.

In a nutshell, "Quiet Time" is indeed a time you as a Christian and believer in Christ Jesus spend alone with God on one to one basis without the interference of the third human party.

Chapter Two

Disciplinary Principles for a Quiet Timer

In order to maintain consistency and personal discipline in ensuring that "Quiet Time" is observed, the following set of suggested rules could be adopted, adapted to and imbibed:

First: No Quiet Time, No Breakfast

> *... the Kingdom of God is not a matter of eating and drinking, but of righteousness, peace and joy in the Holy Spirit.* [Rom. 14:17, NIV]

As such, it should be imbibed as a lifestyle not to have your physical meal in a day, until you have observed quiet time and eaten spiritual meal — ***the word of God.***

If this is done, then you would be fulfilling the Acid Test of making God first, in the list of your priority or above fleshly desire. As you endeavour to do this, your life will experience abundance of God's grace, wisdom, power and riches being administered unto you from His heavenly store house.

Second: Personal Talk with God Before, Man

Making God the priority entails having Him as number one in your daily agenda which includes your daily discussion, conversation or chatting. As such, it is worthwhile making it a rule for you not to have a talk with any man until you have had one with the Almighty in your Quiet Time. Even, if it means just to say "Thank You God" etc., etc.

> *My voice shalt thou hear in the morning, O Lord.* [Psm. 5:3]

Third: Time spent with God before any with man

A daily appointment and time spent with God, before any spent with man attracts the flow of God's favour, nourishment and blessings to your spirit, soul, body and endeavours on a daily basis. So, it is the most ideal act of Godliness for you to make it a point of duty to begin every day with your time spent with the Most High God who makes all things beautiful [Eccl. 3:11], before you spend it with any person. This is a single honour and pleasure for which you were created [Rev. 4:11].

Fourth: Waking up early before others

'Quiet Time'a the term denotes, portrays privacy. It is a time of privacy with God, without allowance for any distraction. As such, it is expected for it to be observed in a noiseless environment and most especially before dawn, when people are still in bed. Therefore, it is expected of a ***'Quiet Time'***to compulsorily make it a duty to wake up early enough, before others in his/her nuclear family hostel, residence and its environs in order to have a time of real privacy with God. This is to say, if others within and around him/her (you) wake up as early as 5.30 a.m., he/she (you) should endeavour to wake up as early as 4.30 a.m, so that, at least an hour could be spent alone with God before any other activities for the day.

Note: A solitary place within your living place or outside your apartment could also be used for your Quiet Time - a time alone with the Almighty.

Fifth: Quiet Time before family altar

It is also better to observe your 'Quiet Time' (a time alone with God) before the hour for your family altar which is a time you spend together with your family members for daily devotion.

The rationale for this principle is to start your day with God, because a day that you start alone with God gives a full refreshing of God's power, anointing, joy and assurance to your spirit, soul and body thus preparing you victoriously for anything that the day has in stock.

Also, by observing your Quiet Time first, you would have had God prepare you on "one-on-one" basis before the congregational one with your family which if not observed first, might not leave you with any extra-lime for its observation before you go out for your daily work.

Nonetheless, observing 'Quiet Time' before your family altar also goes a long way to preparing you ahead of time to be a blessing to other members involved in the family altar.

As such, it is suggested that you adopt this dynamic principle and you will have everything to gain and nothing to lose by it.

Note: In addition to daily "Quiet Time' which you observe in your home, Time of Quietness can as well be observed away from home, in a solitary place and, could last for as long as a man (you) desires. To some, persons, it can be as long as forty days. An example is our Lord and Master, Jesus Christ (Matthew 4:1- 2a; Luke 4:1-2a), and it could be for a day or more, subject to how a person is led to waiting on God and for what purpose.

Chapter Three

Motive for Quiet Time

> *A FALSE balance (Hebrew - Balances of deceit) isabàmination to the Lord: But a just weight is his delight* [Prov. 11:1]

Right, pure, selfless and Godly motive is expected to be the basis for a meaningful acceptable and profitable Quiet Time. If this is not allowed to be the foundation, it will only amount to an 'exercise in futility'. Hence the issue of motive has to be well tackled as an ingredient for a faultless foundation, before delving into the nucleus [the central part around which our subject collects or from which it grows] of 'Quiet Time'.

> *if the foundations [are faulty] be destroyed what can the righteouz do?* [Psm. 11:23]

James in his general epis4e wrote to corroborate the need for a tight motive in approaching God and as a lifestyle for God's people, saying:

> *Ye ask, and receive not, because ye ask amiss [asking with wrong motive], that ye may consume it upon your lusts [pleasures].*
> [James 4:3]

At this juncture, it is pertinent to conclude that failure to maintain a right and acceptable motive before God is a sheee act of self deception which attracts curses instead of blessings, because God cannot be deceived [Gal. 6:7]. So, to have and maintain the foundational principle of tight motives, the word of God should be the parameter because by it is any action weighed. Therefore, the following factors should be the basis for observing 'Quiet Time':

(i) Love for God.
(ii) Desire to knowing God.
(iii) Desire to pleasing Him.
(iv) Desire to finish your race well.

1. Love for God

"God is love" [1 John 3:8b] and whosoever is born of Him is the same, because like gives birth to like. Being born of God who is love therefore simply means, you as a child of God are an epitome of love. As such, to love is your responsibility and loving God becomes your prerogative and it constitutes the primary reason why you were created. Hence He Himself made it a point of duty to shed His love abroad in your heart by the Holy Ghost [Roman 5:5].

Nonetheless, love is the fulfilment of law and it is what makes our Christian faith work and produce results. Hence, it is written: *"... in Jesus Christ, neither circumcision availethany thing, nor uncircumcision; but* ***faith which worketh*** **by *low*"** [Gal. 5:6].

Love, which is the bedrock of Christian faith must therefore be your motivating factor for observing your
'Quiet Time'. When you have it as your motive, heaven
will sanction your efforts and yours will be an exercise in fruitfulness and not in futility.

(ii) Desire to knowing God

Bible says, *'A man of knowledge increaseth strength"* [Prov. 24:5b] and the people that do know their God, shall be strong and do exploits [Dan. 11:32]. As such, desire to knowing God on a progressive basis should complement that of the Love of God as a motivating factor for observing 'Quiet Time'.

When this forms the basis for observing your ***'Quiet Time',*** God will make Himself manifest unto you by His pirit, because the desire will spur you into a sincere, and diligent seeking and searching for all that the scriptures reveal about His Person, without being aechanical about it.

> ... *Ye shall seek me, and find me, when ye shall search for me with all your heart.* [Jer. 29:13]

iii. Desire to please God

Another good and acceptable heart that any child of God should maintain before venturing into observing "Quiet Tine' should include, ***"desire* to *pleasing Cod"***.

> *Delight thyself also in the LORD; and he shall give thee the desires of thine heart.* [Psm. 37:4]

iv. Desire to finish your race well

Time to Observe Quiet Time

There is no stringent rule as regards a time to observe our 'Quietness'. A time and period chosen is a unilateral right and responsibility of your person. In other words, you have the right of choosing a time most sañtable for you far the exercise.

However, in order to make God first on the list of your priority as well as beginning your day with Him early in the morning quite before dawn is considered to be the most appropriate time.

King David is pictured to have his own 'Quiet Time' observed early in the morning as revealed in his own account in the book of Psalm, chapter 5, verses 1 to 3 saying:

1. "Give ear to my words, O LORD, consider my meditation.
2. Hearken unto the voice of my cry, my King, and my God: for unto thee will pray.
3. ***My voice shall thou hear in the morning,O LORD: In the morning will I direct my prayer unto thee and will look up.***

When you make it a prpctise to make your 'Quiet Time' first before anything or activities of the day, God's graee and peace will be multiplied unto you and you will have every cause to glorify Him and glory Him and His name.

For disciplinary measure on your person, you can make it a rule that :No Quiet Time, No Brekkfast?"

Chapter Four

Acts During Quiet Time

The following constitute the substantial acts of a 'Quiet Time' in the closest:

First	Worship
Second	Thanksgiving
Third	Praise
Fourth	Prayers
Fifth	Scriptural Study
Sixth	Listening to hear from Him

First: Worship

Warship is simply hallowing GocL reverently, extillingHIm and expressing His greatness in ***words*** and ***solemn songs***which should emaliate from the bottom of your stomach [the region from where the living water flows] and the depth of your heart. Of course, it is dealing-darling with God in the spirit – Halleluyah!

> *I will worship toward thy holy temple ... for thy loving kindness and for thy truth: for thou hast magnified thy word above all thy name.* [Psm. 138:2)

Note: Worshipping God from your heart creates anatmosphere of His presence within and around you, and automatically brings down His Shekinah glory. It constitutes one of the major acts in your 'Quiet Time'.

Second: Thanksgiving

This simply means giving thanks. In this act, you are expected to count yoiy blessings one by one and in turn express your gratitude unto God for them, because:

Every good gift and every perfect (free, large, full) gift is from above; it comes down from the Father of all [that gives] light, in [the shining of] whom there can be no variation [rising or setting] or shadow cast by His turning [as in an eclipse]. [James 1:17, The Amplified Bible]

King James Version of the Bible simply states:

Every good gift and every perfect gift is from above, and cometh down from the Father of lights; with whom is no variableness, neither shadow of turning. [James 1:17]

Note: The implication of giving thanks to God is that you acknowledge Him – the Almighty as your source and declaring that to Him and to the Devil and his cohorts, By this, you will attract more of God's favourable disposition toward your person.

Nonetheless, the spiritual significance of thanks- giving *is* that with it you can walk your way through thel gates of the Almighty without hitch.

Enter into his gates with thanksgiving.
[Psm. 100:4a]

Third: Praise

Praise is a spiritual phenomenon which has the efficacy of taking you into the ***Court of the Most High God – the decision making arena in heaven:***

Enter ..; into his courts with praise ...
[Psm. 100:4]

Praise of God comes mostly in songs. It is mostly accompanied with kicking, jumping and some form of ecstatic dancing [dancing in a state of intense delight] by people that engage themselves in it. The Bible calls Praise, "the fruits of our lips" which we are commanded to offer as a sacrifice to our God on a continuous basis.

... Let us offer sacrifice of praise to God continually, that is, ***the fruit of our lips*** *...* [Heb. 13:15]

God desires our praise so much that He envelopes Himself in it, making it His habitation.

Thou [God] art holy, O thou that inhabitest the praises of IsraeL [God's people]. [Psm. 22:3]

It will not be an overstatement to state that it was for the purpose of praising God, He created us.

"Thou art worthy, O Lord, to receive glory and honour and power: for thou hast created all things, and for thy pleasure they are and were created. [Rev. 4:11]

David in his understanding of this good purpose for which he was created wrote, saying:

I will ... praise thy name for thy Loving kindness and for thy truth: for thou hast magnjfled thy word above all thy name.
[Psm. 138:2]

In another place, he says:

I will extol (bless) the LORD at all times; his praise will always be on my lips.
[Psm. 34:1, NIV]

Apart from praise, being the fruit of your lips and the purpose for which yqu are created, it isalso an **effective weapon of warfare in your hand to devastate the kingdoms of darkness, to bind their kings with chains and their noble with fetters of iron; and to execute God's judgement of wrath on them** [Psm. 149:1, 3, 5-9]. [A book titled: ***Supernatural Weapons For Believers' Deliverance***by the author of this monograph gives an elaborate insight to 'Praise' as a tool for Warfare and Deliverance].

Therefore beloved, ***I comend you to the spiritual exercise of praising God which is able to build you unto living your life in the experiential power, glory and victory of the Almighty.***

Fourth: Prayer

Prayer is a dynamic supernatutal exercise that you must engage in during your 'Quiet Time'. It is the power and weapon that moves the hand that upholds the world to perform and act favourably on our behalf.

The importance of prayer was revealed in the person of the ***author***and ***finisher***of our ***faith***, the Lord Jesuswhose earthly ministry was saturated with ***spiritual exercise of prayer.***Before He started His ministry, He spent 40 days of separating Himself to God in ***prayer***[Matt. 4:2]. Early before dawn, He would be out in a solitary place for prayer. In all the evening, he would do the same and remained through the night ***praying***[Luke 6:1, 2]. At the consummation of His ministry, before He could face the despicable and dreadful death on the cross, ***He agonised in prayers***on Mount Olives to the extent thaT His sweat was like greet drops of blood falling down to the ground [Luke 22:39-46].

No wonder that His ministry was associated with tremendous results of unspeakable signs, wonders and miracles unto accomplishment of the purpose for which He was sent into this mundane earth.

Having seen how our perfect Master prayed to accomplish the purpose for which He was created, you and I have bo option, but rather to follow His steps. Yes, you (we) have got to pray, ***all forms of prayers: supplication, intercession, importunity, prayer of faith, prayers of authority, dedication, binding* and *loosing;* and *prayer of warfare.*** Hence, Paul the Apostle in instructing believers on how to be strong in the Lord and in the power of his might, and in counteracting the opponent forces of darkness wrote that we should "pray ... always with ***all prayer***and***supplication***in the spirit .. ." [Eph. 6:18].

The God that you (we) are asked to take your (our) requests to in prayer is the one that answers you (us) by ***terrible things***in righteousness and unto Him, are all flesh mandated to come [Psm. 65:5,2]. Without Him,you can do nothing [John 15:5]. Your help comes from Him alone [Psm. 121:2]. If He doesn't help you, no one else can.

However, the good news is that He is all out to help you. Hence He says, ***"Call upon me in the day of trouble: I will deliver thee, and thou shalt glorify me"*** [Psm. 50:65].

Therefore, I commend you to ***CRYING***unto the LORD with your complaints, asking for His interven-tion, protection, provision, directives and blessings in all areas of your life. ***Pray, travail in it***and ***prevail through prayers.***

Nevertheless, when praying, engage the helper of your infirmities - the *Holy Spirit,* to intercede (pray on your behalf) for you [Rom. 8:26].

Fifth: Study

> *Study to shew thyself approved unto God, a workman that needeth not to be ashamed, rightly dividing the word of truth.* [2 Thn. 2:15]

It is God's command that you should study the word of His power (the Bible) to the point of Himself certifying you fit, reliable and dependable. In other words, while it is primarily incumbent on you to study the scripture, which is given by inspiration of God, and is profitable for doctrine, for reproof, for correction, for instruction in righteousness: that the man of God (you) may be perfect, thoroughly furnished unto all good works" [2 Tim. 3:16.17], your motive should be thrt God might be pleased.

The inference in the above explanation is that God will not pick the Bible for you to study. It is your responsibility and mandate to do so conscientiously until the word of Christ dwell in you richly in all wisdom as injuncted in Colossians chapter 3, verse 16.

It is evident at this junction to state categorically that reading is different from studying. While reading may simply indicate browsing (looking through a book or article) in a casual manner studying is a conscious engagement in learning (a subject) which involves investigation by observation and research (Collins General English Dictionaiy).

With the above understanding of the word, ***Study***, what is required of you in this ingredient of your quietness is that your motive should be to learn by searching through the scriptures and allow the words to be imbibed and retained iuyour heart by fixing your eyes on them [Prov. 3:3; 4:20-21].

> *Search the scriptures; for in them ye ... have eternal life: and they are they which testify of me.* [John 5:39]

In essence, studying the scripture goes beyond just reading it, to committing the same into your memory and subsequently into your heart. When the word gets into your heart and is retained, that is when faith has come on your inside by the reason of tbe word [Rom. 10:17; Heb. 4:2].

However, in scriptura1 studies, your motive should be to having a progressive knowledge of God as earlier treated in chapter 3, under Motives for Quietness, because the Bible is the ***living book***that both testifies and gives the true picture of God Person to us:

> *For therein is the righteousness of God revealed from faith to faith.* [Rom. 1:17]

Nonetheless, when studying, you should do so by acknowledging the person of the Holy Spirit who is the inspirator and the teacher of the word. He is in you and by you to explain and reveal the mysteries of the written word to you [2 Pet. 1:20-21].

Subsequently it is the Spirit that reveals the things that are freely given to you in Christ Jesus via the word; whom you are in Him and the things that are expected of you as God's child, son or daughter.

Note:When you are filled with the knowledge of the word of God in all wisdom, you will be powerful and strong in Him to do exploits and no one shall be able to question your authority [Col. 3:16; Dan. 11:32; Eccl. 8:4].

> *Beloved, I commend you to God and to the word of his grace, which is able to build you up, and to give you an inheritance among, all them which are sanctified.* [Acts 20:32]

Sixth: Meditation in the Word

Literarily, meditation means to reflect deeply especially on spiritual matters. So, to meditate in the word of God simply means to have a ***deep thought***or ***a deep reflection***on the word of God which lives and abides forever (1 Pet. 1:23).

Unfortunately, it is in this area of spiritual labour that God's' people fail. Reason for the failure is attributed to threeinainfactor,, viz:

(a) Lack of personal discipline to give oneself to meditation.
(b) Lack of personal commitment to God.
(c) ack of dedication to God and His word.

However, meditation in the word is the. most noble, most lifting and most rewarding discipline that any child of God can ever engage in. This importance of meditation was revealed in God's command to Joshua, after he had been chosen to succeed Moses in leading the Israelites (God's people) to the promised land thus:

> *This book of the law shall not depart out of thy mouth; but thou sholt MEDITATE therein day and night, that thou mayest observe to do ,according to all that is written therein: For then thou shalt make thy way prosperous, and then thou shalt have good success.* [Josh. 1:8]

At this juncture, it is pertinent to state that it is important and of more value to judiciously spend time meditating On a verse of the scriptures than just reading through a whole chapter of it.

METHODOLOGY FOR MEDITATION

A. Recognition of the Holy Spirit as a Teacher

You need to hold tenaciously unto the scriptural truth about the Person of the Holy Spirit, who could be referred to as the author of the scriptures, for the revealing fact that He ***inspired***the Prophets ofold to putdown the written words [LOGOS], that is, the Bible:

As such, it implicit that He has the sole mandate to explicate the ***truth***and reveal the mysteries (spirit behind the letter) unto you [2 Cor. 3:6; Matt. 13:11].

Apart from being the inspirator of the word, Holy Spirit is the third Person of God-head that the Father [God] sent in the name of Jesus to ***teach***you all things – the scripture; being the number one, and to bring all things to your remembrance [John 14:26]. The same Spirit is in you to teach you all things, called the truth [1 Coe 12:3; 1 John 2:20, 27].

With this understanding, each time you open your Bible to study, you should endeavour to do so in the consciousness of a student (which you are] in a formal classroom, seated before a Teacher [The Holy Spirit], from whom you will learn.

B. Choose a verse to study

With the first method above as the bedrock, choose a
verse to study, e.g. Gospel according to Saint John, chapter 1 and verse 12.

C. Study the Verse in toto

In studying the verse, you will first need to have a literary understanding of every word, phrase, sentence and the general statement of the verse.

D. Meditation/Retention

Subsequently, commit every word, phrase, sentence and general statement of the verse to deep thinking, which is known as ***MED ITATION.*** As you do this, some indepth meaning, beyond the literary one that you have had will begin to emanate or erupt from your innermost being jiyour spirit man]. That indepth meaning is. what is called ***REVELATION-KNOWLEDGE.***

Anyway, while you are thinking deep on the verse of the scripture, it is also expected of you to bear the word, phrase, sentences and the entire scriptural passage in mind, by committing each to your memory. Thereafter, consciously allow same to go into your heart, that is, internalise the word.

When this has been done, all you will need to do at any other time is simply meditating on the words and verse of the scriptures which you have already retained in your heart without necessarily opening the page of the Bible any longei; because it is already registered on the table of your heart. This is what will make meditation on the word easier for you to do at any point in time and in any place without an outward display of any kind, that could portray a religious show.

Having meditated and received an insight ***[Rhema]***into the written word ***[LOGOS]***you will then need to appropriate the word.

APPROPRIATING THE WORD is taking time word for yourself, e.g. in

> *as many as received him, to them gave power to become the sons of God even to them that believe in his name.* [John 1:12]

you will simply put it thus: "I have received Him and have therefore been given power to become the son of God, even me that have believed on his name."

Subsequently, ***PRAY THE WORD:***Having had the word in you, the next step to take is to pray the word for it to become part and parcel of you, as well as asking for more grace and strength; based on the word from God, to enable you become a doer of the same [the word].

> *Wherefore lay apart all filthiness and superfluity of naughtiness, and receive with meekness the engrafted*

word, which is able to save your souls. ... But be ye doers of the word, and nor hearers only, deceiving your own selves. [James 1:21, 22]

Seventh: Hearing From God

The Living God, whom we serve does not only desire to hear us speak to Him, He delights even more in speaking to us. However, it is most unfortunate that many of God's people only speak to God, but do not know how to hear from Him and as such have never heard from Him. Such have eyes, they cannot see what the Spirit is revealing. They have ears, they cannot hear what the Spirit is saying to the Church.

However, hearing God constitutes a very important issue in our walking relationship with God, and particularly in the period of 'Quiemess' with Him.

God's delights in speaking to lead us are exemplified in the following scriptures:

> *I will instruct thee and teach thee in the way which thou shalt go; I will guide thee with mine eyes.* [Psm. 32:8]

Jesus spoke aloud that:

> *I am the light of the world; he that followeth me shall not walk in darkness, but shall have the light of life.* [John 8:12]

There's nothing that can beat being led of God by heating Him in all areas of our lives:

> *The steps of a good man are ordered by the LORD: and he ddighteth in his way.* [Psm. 37:23]

He Himself says:

> *I am the LORD thy God which teacheth thee to profit, which leadeth thee by the way that thou shouldest go.* [Is. 48:17]

Because

... the way of a man is not in himself: it is not in man that walketh to direct his steps. [Jer. 10:23)

Nonetheless, to be led of God and hear from Him requires your absolute trust in Him. You must also crave to having Him instruct you as well as maintaining a position of watching and listening to hearing what He will say to you. Hence it is written:

Thust in the LORD with all thine heart; and lean not unto thine own understanding. In all thy ways acknowledge him, and he shall direct thy paths. [Prov. 3:5]

Habakuk's attitude in the closet to hearing from God as accounted by Him is a typical model of the position to mantain in order to have the same experience of receiving God's instruction:

I will stand upon my watch, and set upon the tower and will swatch to see what he will say unto me, and What I shall answer when I am reproved. [Hab. 2:1]

Habakuk's attitude in maintaining a disciplined waiting position until he hears God speak to him is glaring.

In verse 2 of the chapter, he says,

... the LORD answered me and said, write the vision and make it plain upon tables, that he may run that readeth it.

The ***First***lesson to learn from Habakuk's experience is that God answers every heart cry that is directed to Him. God answered him.

Second: God speaks to His own. "God said" (spoke) to him what to do.

Third: God gives focus and insight on what to do to HIis own. In Habakuk's case, God gave him vision him accomplished in life.

However, it is pertinent to state at this junction that waiting to hear from God is in two terms, viz:

(a) The short term period of waiting.

(b) The long term period.

(a)* The *short term periodinvolves a very short period of concentrated waiting on God in absolute silence to hearfrom Him. The periodis usually elastic that it will not be prudent to condine it to a time certain or limit. Largely, the short period is still subject
to the issue that one desires to receive God's instruction on. To this extent, the shortest period of waiting can be between the period of 15 and 30 minutes out of the time earmarked for the spiritual exercises of Quiet Time.

Nevertheless, the level of your sincenty in focus and concentration in waiting on God without enter- taining any form of distraction will go a long way to determine how long the short period of waiting to hearing from Him will be.

(b) Subsequently, just as the name connotes, ***long term period*** of waiting and listening to hear from God involves a long period of patiently waiting on God until one hears Him speak to him with particular reference to one's demand from Him. Here the period lasts as long as one lasts in this mundane world, relatively to the gravity of what the person needs to hear from God for, coupled with how a person submits his or her total life to the Most High God.

It is pertinent at this junction to advise that you surrender your whole being and subject every issue of your life to God's instruction and leadership before you make a decision and or take steps on the same. In fact, this is God's utmost desire for His people, that is, to direct and give them (you) direction on every issue of their (your) lives (life), so that the decision taken by them (you) will be prudent and guaranteed of good success. Hence it is written that:

> *... thine ears shall hear a word behind thee, saying, This is the way, walk ye in it, when ye turn to the right hand, and when ye turn to the left.* [Isaiah 30:21]

The instruction from the Most High God therefore:

Give ear, and hear my voice, hearken and hear my speech. [Isaiah 28:23]

The Most High went ahead through His Prophet, saiah, to ask the following questions:

Doth the plowman plow all day to sow? Doth he open and break the clods of his ground? When he hath made plain the face of it, doth he not cast abroad the dill; and scatter the cummin, and cast in the wheat in rows; and the appointed barely and the spelt in their place? For his God doth instruct him to discretion and doth teach him. [Isaiah 28:24-26]

Beloved reader; God teaches and instructs His children a discretion. Therefore, let Him be your ***Teacher*** and *'nstructor*so that undaunted discretion can be your oortion.

Nonetheless, both ***the short*** and ***long terms*** of hearing from God requires a deliberate effort on your oart, to be still [absent from and silent to ***self*** as well is maintaining quietness] before God; and surrenderly allow Him to have His say to you. Hence, He Himself says:

Be still and know that I am God. [Psm. 46:10]

Chapter Five

How God Speaks to His Own (You)

There are numerous ways by which God Speaks to every son or daughter of His. However, we shall briskly examine the following only.

First - By the Word: Priniary way by which God speaks to us is via the scriptures. In other yords, whatever the word says is what God says.

Second - By the Holy Spirit:[Acts 13:1; 1 Tim. 4:1; John 16:13] God also speaks to us by His ***Spirit***who transmits God's messages into our spirit-man from where it is in turn taken over by our mind where the messages are logically put together and Later vocalised or expressed by us through our vocal organ.

Third - By His Angel:God also speaks to us by sending His Angels to deliver divine messages to us, as in the case of Cornelius. a centurion of the Italian band as recorded in the Acts of the Apostles chapter 10 and verses 1 to 7.

Fourth - Via Trance:Trance is another means by which God speaks to us. Here, our senses are suspended, while we are not at a sleeping state and things are revealed to us in the realm of the spirit. I had such an experiencc in the year 1990, in Oko, Anambra State, in the eastern part of Nigeria. On this fateful day, I knelt down to pray at ahout 6.00 p.m. in the evening to round up my fasting for the day, when I suddenly saw in a trance, my aunty-in-law who resides in Kaduna, in the northern part of Nigeria who sat at the back of a 504 Peugeot car painted green, very sick and about to be driven down to the hospital. The experience was so real as if I was physically present at her place in Kaduna. However, it was clearly indicated that God simply wanted me to know what was going on with her so that I could pray on her behalf, which I earnestly did with my prayer partner.

Another example could be found in Peter the Apostle's trance-experience in the Acts of Apostles, chapter 10 and verses 9 to 16.

Fifth – By Inner Still Voice: [Rom. 8:16] We hear God speak to us by our inner still voice. This sometimes comes by deep, positive and Godly impression on our hearts. At other times, it comes in a still small voice, especially at our resting period, when we are not preoccupied with our body organs.

Sixth – Via Dream:God also does speak to us via dream. But it is very relevant and important to state here that we need to be filled with the knowledge of God so much that we do not fall into an error of receiving the enemy's message through this medium for God's, because this medium is equally uset by the Devil.

Seventh – Via Vision:Vision is another important medium through which God speaks to us. It could be through an *OPEN VISION* where you may not be sleeping but yet suddenly transmute into the realm of the spirit by an act of Gqd, to see and receive what he [God] would want you to receive. It is somehow in the form of trance.

Nonetheless, it could also be through a *NIGHT VISION.* Here, God makes you see and bear things live, as durinj the day and of course, with an understanding of what the thing is, which will be committed to your memory so much that you will never forget it after you are up from your steep. A lot of people mistake this for 'dream' because it occurs while alseep, during the course of the night.

Chapter Six

Benefits Accredited to You As A Quiet Timer

1. You will know God, His Power, Might, Majesty and Supremacy [Rom. 1:17].
2. You will be strong in Him and do exploit [Dan. 11:32b].
3. You will be sound, bold, confident and be of goad courage [2 Tim. 1:7; Heb. 10:35; Josh. 1:6].
4. You will become powerful in Him and your authority will be unquestionable [Eccl. 8:4].
5. You will be knowledgeable [John 8:31,32).
6. You will increase in the strength of God [Prov.24:5c).
7. You will become great [Jer. 5:5ab].
8. You will become God's favourite [Prov. 3:3,4; Is. 66:5).
9. God's guarantee of welfare and security shall be yours [Jer. 1:18,19].
10. Those who gather against you shall fall for your sake [Is. 54:15].
11. Those who are incensed against you shall be put to shame [Is. 45:24b].
12. No weapon fashioned against you shall prosper [Is. 54:17a].
13. You will condemn any tongue that rises against you injudgement [Is. 54:17b].
14. The Lord will be with you always as a mighty terrible one [Jer. 20:11].
15. Your persecutors shall stumble and be ashamed [Jer. 20:11].
16. Your persecutors shall not prosper and everlasting confusion shall be their portion [Jer. 20:11].
17. Whatsoever you lay your hands upon shall prosper [Psm. 1:3].
18. You shall have good success [Josh. 1:8].
19. You shall be blessed and be a blessing [Gen. 12:2].

20. You shall be like a tree planted by the rivers of water [Psm. 1:3].
21. Your end shall be better than your beginning [Eccl. 7:8].
22. Surely, goodness and mercy shall follow you all the days of your life [Psm. 23:6].

www.ingramcontent.com/pod-product-compliance
Lightning Source LLC
LaVergne TN
LVHW020537160826
845677LV00015B/4108
9798846441392